READY, SET, DRAW!
SUPERHEROES

AILIN CHAMBERS

Gareth Stevens
PUBLISHING

Please visit our website, **www.garethstevens.com**. For a free color catalog of all our high-quality books, call toll free 1-800-542-2595 or fax 1-877-542-2596.

Library of Congress Cataloging-in-Publication Data

Chambers, Ailin.
Superheroes / by Ailin Chambers.
p. cm. — (Ready, set, draw!)
Includes index.
ISBN 978-1-4824-0930-7 (pbk.)
ISBN 978-1-4824-0926-0 (6-pack)
ISBN 978-1-4824-0929-1 (library binding)
1. Heroes in art — Juvenile literature. 2. Drawing — Technique — Juvenile literature. I. Chambers, Ailin. II. Title.
NC825.H45 C43 2015
743.4—d23

First Edition

Published in 2015 by
Gareth Stevens Publishing
111 East 14th Street, Suite 349
New York, NY 10003

Editors: Samantha Hilton, Kate Overy and Joe Harris
Illustrations: Dynamo Limited
Design concept: Keith Williams
Design: Dynamo Limited and Notion Design
Cover design: Ian Winton

Printed in the United States of America

CPSIA compliance information: Batch #CS15GS: For further information contact Gareth Stevens, New York, New York at 1-800-542-2595.

CONTENTS

GRAB THESE!

Are you ready to create some amazing pictures? Wait a minute! Before you begin drawing, you will need a few important pieces of equipment.

PENCILS

You can use a variety of drawing tools, such as pens, chalks, pencils, and paints. But to begin use an ordinary pencil.

PAPER

Use a clean sheet of paper for your final drawings. Scrap paper is useful and cheap for your practice work.

ERASERS

Everyone makes mistakes! That's why every artist has a good eraser. When you erase a mistake, do it gently. Erasing too hard will ruin your drawing and possibly even rip it.

RULER

Always use a ruler to draw straight lines.

COMPASS

You can use a compass to draw a perfect circle, but it can be tricky at first. Try tracing a coin, bottle top, or any other small, round item you can find.

PENS

The drawings in this book have been finished with an ink line to make them sharper and cleaner. You can get the same effect by using a ballpoint or felt-tip pen.

PAINT

Adding color to your drawing brings it to life. You can use felt-tip pens, colored pencils, or water-based paints such as poster paints, which are easy to clean.

GETTING STARTED

In this book we use a simple two–color system to show you how to draw a picture. Just remember: New lines are blue lines!

STARTING WITH STEP 1

The first lines you will draw are very simple shapes. They will be shown in blue. You should draw them with a normal pencil.

ADDING MORE DETAIL

As you move on to the next step, the lines you have already drawn will be shown in black. The new lines for that step will appear in blue.

FINISHING YOUR PICTURE

When you reach the final stage, you will see the image in full color with a black ink line. Inking a picture means tracing the main lines with a black pen. After the ink dries, use your eraser to remove all the pencil lines before adding your color.

The method shown on the left is perfect if you want to draw a character in the same pose every time. But what if you want to draw the same character in lots of different poses?

STEP 1: START WITH A STICKMAN

Place a piece of paper over a character you like and trace it as a stickman. How big or long are the arms, legs, head, and body?

STEP 2: STRIKE A POSE!

Draw a new stickman in a different position, making sure that the arms, legs, head, and body are exactly the same size as in your first traced picture.

STEP 3: ACTION!

Now, you can flesh out your character in the new pose. Once you are happy with what you have drawn in pencil, add colors.

THE FIREFLY

The Firefly is a bug-eyed hero with amazing fire powers. Flames leap out from his body!

STEP 1

First, copy these shapes to create his head, torso, and pelvis.

STEP 2

Next, add these long, thin shapes for his arms and thighs.

STEP 3

Give your superhero a pointy chin, clenched fists, and curved lower legs.

STEP 4

Now, add the flames. You can also draw muscles on his upper arms. Add two lines to join his torso and underwear.

STEP 5

Then draw two big
eyes, and add a flame
pattern to his chest.

STEP 6

Finally, bring your hero to life
by adding flames to his head.
Use bright colors, such as
yellow and red, for his body.

MISS MIRACLE

With her long, flowing cape, Miss Miracle is ready to fly into action. She keeps her true identity a secret with her green eye mask.

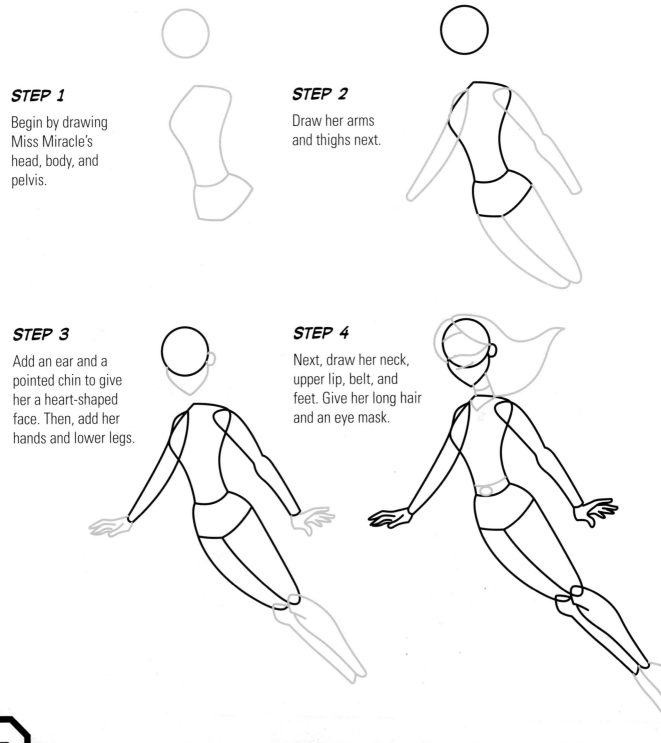

STEP 1

Begin by drawing Miss Miracle's head, body, and pelvis.

STEP 2

Draw her arms and thighs next.

STEP 3

Add an ear and a pointed chin to give her a heart-shaped face. Then, add her hands and lower legs.

STEP 4

Next, draw her neck, upper lip, belt, and feet. Give her long hair and an eye mask.

STEP 5

Now, add the details to her face and clothes. Don't forget her flowing cape.

STEP 6

Enjoy coloring Miss Miracle. Color the details on her clothes in a different shade to make them stand out.

WHIZZ-KID

You don't have to be a grown-up to be a superhero. Whizz-Kid is a teenager who can move with lightning speed.

STEP 1

First, draw a peanut shape for her torso, then a circle for her head.

STEP 2

Next, add carrot shapes for her upper arms and thighs.

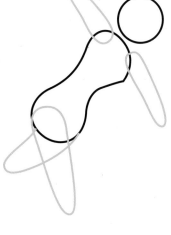

STEP 3

Add her chin and ear. Then, draw her lower arms and legs to make it look as if she's racing to the rescue.

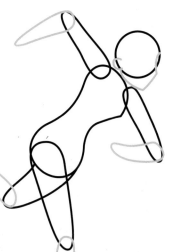

STEP 4

Draw her feet, hands, neck, hair, and eyes. Then, add other details to her outfit, as shown here.

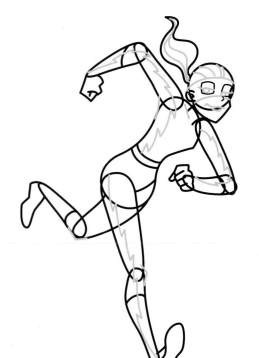

STEP 5

Finish sketching her face, eye mask, and hair. Add sharp, jagged lines to her costume.

STEP 6

Don't forget to draw lines and puffs of smoke to show that she's zooming into action. Then, color her however you like.

SUPER TIP!

Puffs of smoke show sudden movement. They are easy to draw:

- In pencil, draw circles of different sizes. Overlap them until you have the shape and size of puff you want.

- Ink around the edge of the shape. Then erase the inner parts to finish your puff of smoke.

DOC PARADOX

This evil scientist spends all day in his laboratory thinking of nasty ways to take over the world. His latest invention, the Impossi-tron, might help him do just that!

STEP 1

Start by drawing Doc's lab coat.

STEP 2

Next, add a big, round head, sleeves and pants.

STEP 3

Now, draw his ear, big chin, hands, and feet.

STEP 4

Next, draw his crazy hair. Then, add his neck, the front of his lab coat, and the bottom of the Impossi-tron.

STEP 5

Next, draw Doc's crazy eyes and his face. Add the details to his shirt, and the rest of the Impossi-tron.

STEP 6

Draw energy waves coming from the top of the Impossi-tron. Then, color Doc. You could add a faint scar on this head, too.

CAPTAIN FANTASTIC

Captain Fantastic has everything a superhero needs. He's got super strength, super speed, and a really super hairstyle.

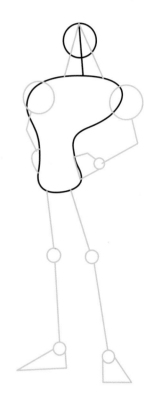

STEP 1

First, draw his wide body and head. Then, add a vertical line to find the center of his head and neck. This will help you get everything in the right place.

STEP 2

Draw two more lines from the top of his head to make a triangle. Then, add his arms, legs, and feet.

STEP 3

Complete the arms, and start to flesh out his legs. Add a mop of hair and a strong chin. Draw his belt and a line to form the bottom of his cape.

STEP 4

Draw the rest of his cape. Add the eye mask, shins, and sloping shoulders.

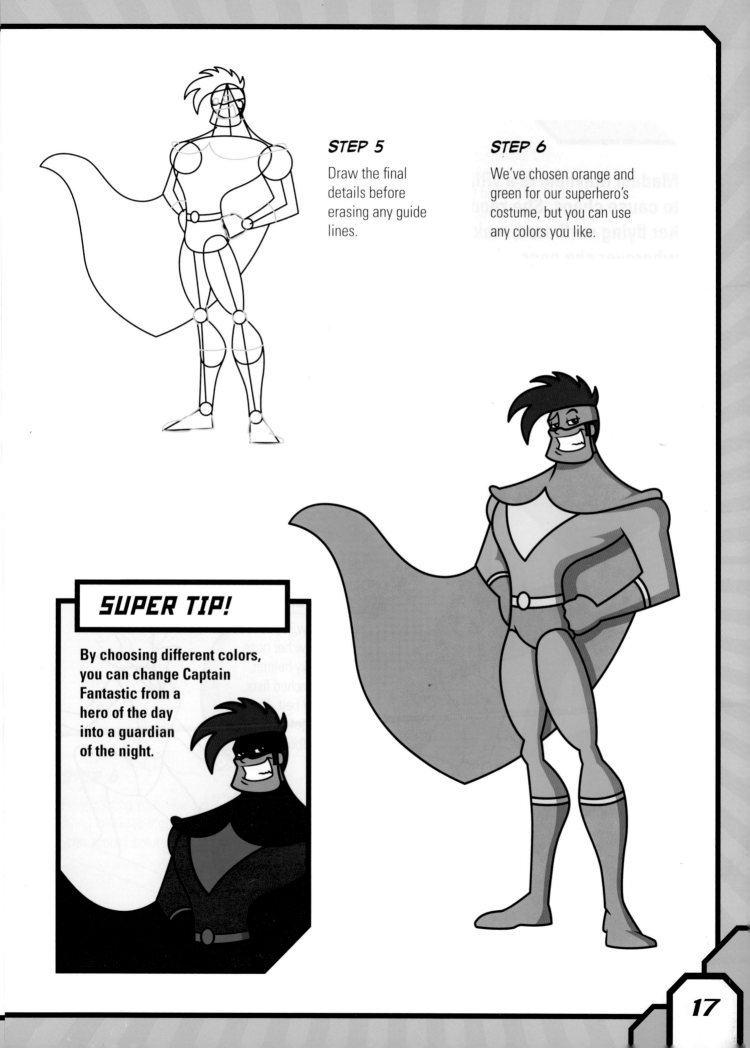

STEP 5

Draw the final details before erasing any guide lines.

STEP 6

We've chosen orange and green for our superhero's costume, but you can use any colors you like.

SUPER TIP!

By choosing different colors, you can change Captain Fantastic from a hero of the day into a guardian of the night.

17

THE BLUE DRAGON

The Blue Dragon looks strong and fearsome! He has sharp wings on his head and legs. Even his cape looks like a dragon's wing. Draw him if you dare!

STEP 1

First, draw the Blue Dragon's torso and pelvis. Don't forget his egg-shaped head!

STEP 2

Add his muscular arms and thighs.

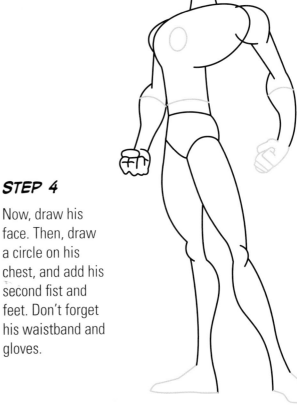

STEP 3

Draw his neck to join his head and body together. Add his lower legs, and finish his arms before adding one clenched fist.

STEP 4

Now, draw his face. Then, draw a circle on his chest, and add his second fist and feet. Don't forget his waistband and gloves.

STEP 5

Add his mask and the wings of the symbol on his chest. The wings on his head and legs have the same curved edge as his cape.

STEP 6

Use lots of different shades of blue to color your Blue Dragon.

CAPTAIN TWILIGHT

As night falls, Captain Twilight uses his magical powers to fight crime. He swoops down, wrapped in a large, purple cloak.

STEP 1

Begin by drawing Captain Twilight's head, torso, and pelvis.

STEP 2

Next, draw his arms and thighs using these long, thin shapes.

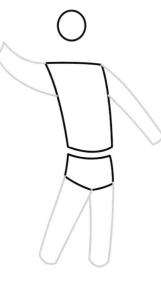

STEP 3

Draw his chin, hands, and lower legs. Make the larger hand open, and don't join it to the wrist.

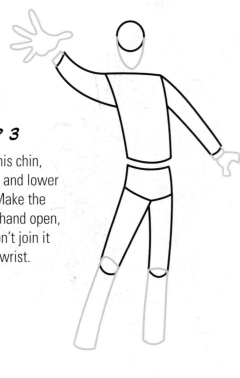

STEP 4

Give your hero a top hat. Then, draw some puffy clouds for him to stand on.

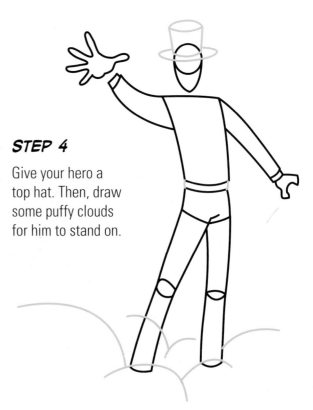

Captain Twilight's mystical powers are easy to show by following these steps:

- Add a wavy line around the hand, but not actually touching it.

- Add a second wavy line just outside the first.

- You can add dots and stars to make a sparkling effect.

STEP 5

Draw his eyes and mouth, as well as the details of his clothes and cloak. Add some more clouds.

STEP 6

Complete your picture by drawing a magical glow around his open hand. Then color him with dark, mysterious colors.

THE CRUNCHER

This metal-jawed villain is very mean. The Cruncher's powerful body and deadly jaws will crush anything in sight!

STEP 1

First, draw his big torso and his pelvis. Add a small circle for his head.

STEP 2

Then, draw his chunky arms and thighs.

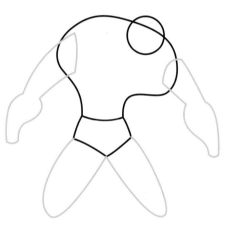

STEP 3

Next, finish the legs of his jeans, and add a belt buckle. Draw clenched fists before adding his metal jaws.

STEP 4

Now, give him spiky hair, and add the details to his clothes.

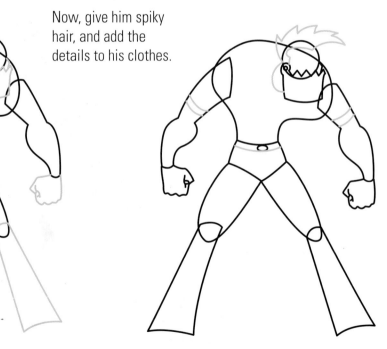

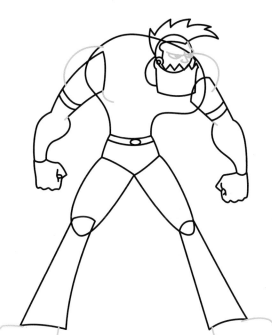

STEP 5

Draw his face, giving him a heavy brow to make him look mean. Then, add bulging arm muscles and big feet.

STEP 6

Now, you can add color. Use shading to show off his large chest and arm muscles.

GALAXY GIRL

Galaxy Girl is a daring space traveler.
Armed with a cosmic wand, her mission is
to protect the world from an alien attack.

STEP 1

Begin by drawing Galaxy Girl's
head, torso, and thighs.

STEP 2

Next, draw her arms and
lower legs, so it looks as
if she's floating in space.

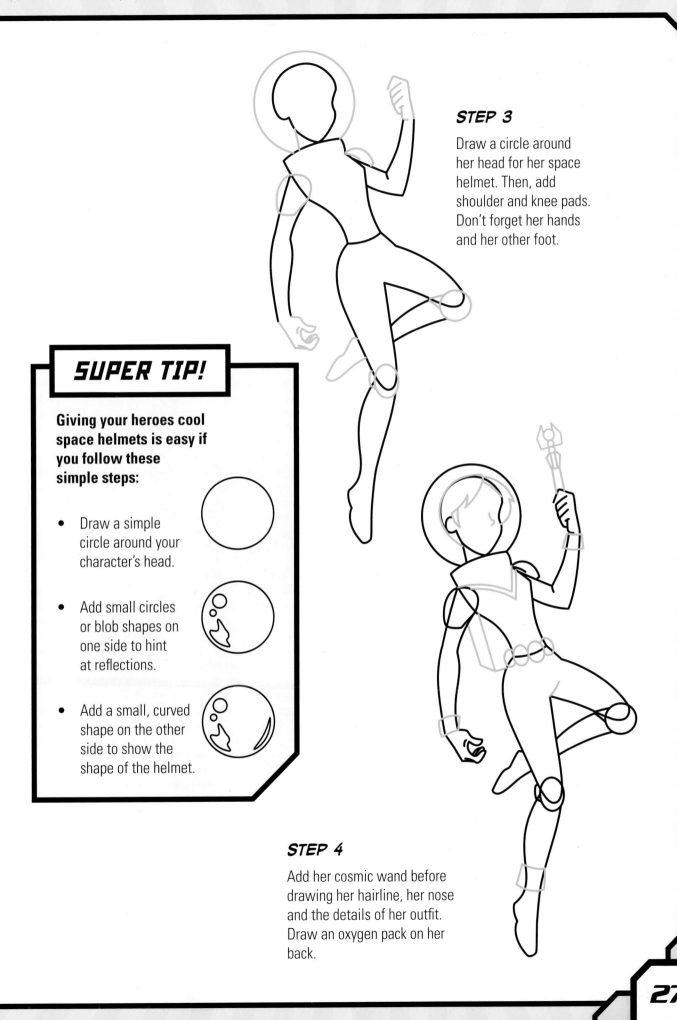

STEP 3

Draw a circle around her head for her space helmet. Then, add shoulder and knee pads. Don't forget her hands and her other foot.

SUPER TIP!

Giving your heroes cool space helmets is easy if you follow these simple steps:

- Draw a simple circle around your character's head.

- Add small circles or blob shapes on one side to hint at reflections.

- Add a small, curved shape on the other side to show the shape of the helmet.

STEP 4

Add her cosmic wand before drawing her hairline, her nose and the details of her outfit. Draw an oxygen pack on her back.

STEP 5

Draw her face and curved breathing tube. Add oval reflection shapes to her helmet. Draw some curved lines to show the cosmic wand sending a signal.

STEP 6

Finally, add some cool colors that will make Galaxy Girl look out of this world!

Rocket Racer wears Rollerblades and a rocket backpack to blast him along at super-speed. He's so fast that bad guys don't even see him coming!

STEP 1

Draw a rounded shape like a balloon for his head. Add his torso and pelvis.

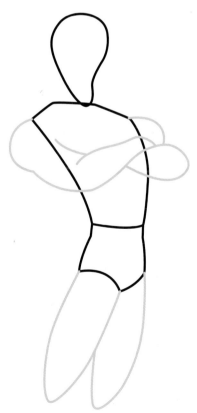

STEP 2

Next, add his thighs and folded arms.

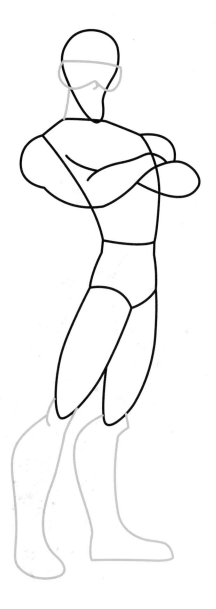

STEP 3

Add a line for his neck. Then, draw a large pair of goggles and muscular lower legs.

STEP 4

Draw his helmet fin, and add the straps for his backpack. Then, begin to draw his Rollerblades.

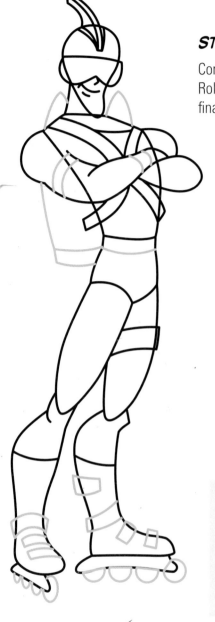

STEP 5

Complete his backpack and Rollerblades. Then, add the final details to his costume.

STEP 6

Use bright red and yellow details to bring your hero to life.

10-14

GLOSSARY

brow Forehead.

compass An instrument for drawing circles.

laboratory A place where scientists do experiments.

mystical Mysterious and fascinating.

pelvis The bony frame at the base of the spine to which the legs are attached.

torso The trunk of the human body—from the neck to the pelvis.

vertical Up and down (rather than sideways).

FURTHER READING

Superhero Doodles for Kids by Chris Sabatino (Gibbs M.Smith Inc., 2012)

Superheroes by Ted Rechlin (Dover Children's, 2012)

WEBSITES

www.hellokids.com/r_484/coloring-pages/super-heroes-coloring-pages

www.how-to-draw-cartoons-online.com/cartoon-superheroes.html

www.my-how-to-draw.com/how-to-draw-spiderman.html

INDEX